1995
NEW
H9

My Mind's Eye

Poetry and Visual Art on
Social Justice, Philosophy and Identity.

Topaz Hooper

To my mother and father

who have always taught me to do the right thing and good
things will happen.

table
of contents

Chapters

BONUS

40

05

52

18

Paintings

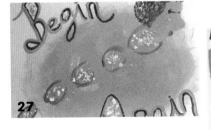
27

09

66

IT'S TOUGH HAVING A NAME LIKE TOPAZ:

IT'S SO UNIQUE THAT YOU KNOW NO ONE
ELSE ON THE SCHOOL ROSTER
HAS IT BUT SO ALIEN THAT YOU'LL NEVER
FIND IT ON A COKE BOTTLE OR
A MINI LAS VEGAS LICENSE PLATE.
SO DEGENDERED
THAT EVEN TELEPHONE OPERATORS DON'T
KNOW WHETHER TO CALL ME
SHE, HE, ZE, OR THEY.
SO EXTRAVAGANT THAT
EVEN THE MOST "DIVERSIFIED" CORPORATE
ENVIRONMENTS CAN'T EVEN FATHOM IT.
TO BE A TOPAZ IS TO BE A GEM
EMULSIFIED BY THE MOST INTENSE
PRESSURE FROM ITS ENVIRONMENT WITH
THE CAPACITY TO STILL CATCH A LIGHT AND
SHINE THROUGH THE DARK

INTRODUCTION

I dedicate this book of rhymes to those who value the power of poetry.

Those who declare defiantly that poetry is not simply for entertainment. Nor is poetry simply an aesthetic; that which we see exemplified on the back of Christmas cards.

This book is for those who are certain poetry can move the masses. Poetry can change the hearts and minds of those who cannot identify with someone's personal battles yet can understand the need to fight them.

My poetry is designed to fill the minds of the readers with internal dialogue. Some of which I believe should have been happening all along. The kind of dialogue that is critical of what we believe to be true or false, moral or immoral, right or wrong.

Please enjoy this book of poetry as an example of true narratives and experiences from my eyes.

This book of poetry is not fictional, nor fantastical, nor hyperbolic. It is a condensation of my mind's eye that are true and factual to me. Take each word or phrase with a grain of salt and think about where politically you stand.

That, my friends, is the best way to understand.

SELF (LOVE)

THE CAFFEINE DREAM

Mocha
drips
from
my
cup
into
yours

as I write this nonchalant napkin poem. I am mocha and you are the   cup
you cradle my chocolateness and add the caffeine from your   soul.
I scream for cream to infiltrate my mocha, swirls of   temptation
that mix up my world into a dream of spirals and sugary   good-
ness.

MY MINDS EYE

You are so good.

I want to drip mocha into your cup so you can feel my   sweet
interruption. Like ink on a page. Light in cave. Molly at a   rave.
Potatoes with sage. I want to be the mocha to your caffeine   like
a cold stream of ocean tears. Like the way   the
wind ruffles my skirt in a cloud of earth. Let me   be
the mocha to your caffeine. We are the   perfect
combination of smooth and rich.
Let me interrupt your
continuous and make a world of curious.

EARTHLY BEAUTY

I am
beautiful, yes I am.
You may watch, but you
may not touch. My body
is sacred. A place of
religiosity.
I religiously splash papaya water on my skin
And paint my sins with warm shea butter.
My body is delicate. Only walnut seeds and honey
may grace my large follicles. My body and being are
oceanic. Full of the salt in water
But the wildlife is different.
There are no crabs to clamp and cut.
There is no shrimp to feed on my endless bottom.
There is only salmon.
Pink, soft, delicious.
My eyes are almonds with chocolate chip centers.
My hair is as buoyant as young children playing on pogo sticks.
My skin is as rich, brown and red as the Colorado River.
My breasts are soft and juicy mangos.
My hips are bullies that get their way.
My legs are tree trunks
Rooted, firm, and nourished
My feet are made of flowers.
Opening and closing in unison.
My lips are plush pillows of strawberry and banana.

My body is sacred.
Whole. Loved.
By me. And for me.

"Fly Away"
Acrylic on Canvas
2016

BEAUTIFUL

Beautiful, me
Beautiful, you
Me, you, what's the competition about?

Short and stout, smells of sauerkraut
damn, you're beautiful.
High and wide, hairy thighs,
damn, you're beautiful.
Unibrow since 5th grade,
and her mind is sharp as a blade.
You look so good
sometimes I wish we could trade.

But why?
When I was built like a goddess in the sky,
while my curls whip and fly
and my hips don't lie
and my lips taste like raspberry juice.

Stop the competition, let's call it a truce.
You and me baby ain't nothin' but mammalsilites
dark and light can exist together alright.

The hair on your pits,
your large left tit,
the way you hack when you spit
are all parts of beautiful you.

Your broad shoulders,
you head as it gets balder,
your beer gut
and your extra long nut
are all what I love about you.

MY MINDS EYE

You. You. Beautiful you.
Fuck conventional beauty standards
that no one lives up to.

Your lovely split ends,
your spine that bends,
your eyes with crust in the corner
and your uncontrollable morning boner
are all beautiful to me.

Believe it or not,
they're the best thing.
The imperfect human body
in combination with the soul
are way more beautiful
than things I was told.

I'll tell you now,
I love my brown skin
it keeps me protected
with its smooth melanin.
Like the pearly whiteness
of the teeth in my mouth
and the breasts on my chest
that can't help but poke out.
My eyes like almonds
with chocolate chip centers
and behind my mind
holds tons of great treasures.
And my feet hold calves
that give me great pleasure.

So fuck what ya 'hurd.
Tear up those magazines,
each rock and rose are beautiful
and we're fucking amazing.

COMM (UNITY)

"My People"
Acrylic on Wood
2015

TO MY BROTHER

To My Brother

To my brother who begs for change
on the street of Colfax at three in the morning,

I see you.

I reach for the sparse dollar I carry in my knock-off designer purse
and hand it to you without warning,

I see you.

As your eyes glow radioactive green from the
sludge they feed you at McDonald's,
and all of the fake images of white models they compare your life to,
and all of the sparse dollars you will receive tonight,

I see you.

Dear Brother, you were once glorious I know,
your skin with melanin crystals
that glisten in the sun
those days when you were a child
and used to have so much fun
And the day they offered you
your very first gun
And the moment the police saw you
and you had to run.

I see you. I see you. I see you.

Dear Brother, you are not a product of your mistakes.
You are a product of the decisions that the state makes.
Where you live is not your choice,

What you drive, that 1990's Toyota and not that Rolls-Royce.
What you sing is determined by the factors that silenced your voice.
What I hear is not your screaming, but the politics of their noise.

Dear Brother, I see you.
Tattered clothes,
pimpin' hoes,
dreaming of the day
when you can go.

And ski in Aspen just in time for the powdered snow.
Escape to Angola just because you wanted to know.
Fly to Jamaica because the beach holds your soul.
Being black in America is quite the heavy toll.

But Dear Brother, now that I see you,
there's no excuse not to grow to tall.
Be the King of the Jungle as the Amazon falls.

Dear Brother, they cannot see
all of that which you have been told.
They have been blinded by the whiteness
at the end of this road.
But you have seen things that are as old as the Pharaohs.

Calligraphy and graffiti, same thing.
permaculture and urban gardens, same thing.
drive-bys and military airplanes shot from the sky, same thing.
baby mamas and Mormonism in the Utah mountains, same thing.
hustling on the streets and going door-to-door for the next presidential
candidate, same thing.

Do you see dear Brother?
You are gifted I know,
the only thing they can't steal from you
is your will to grow.
But we both know, Bob Marley said, "Kill them before they grow."
But little did they know, we were seeds.

And we will grow as tall as the Amazon trees.
and with each generation, we only grow stronger
until our roots grow thicker and our blood lasts longer.

Dear Brother, I see you.
I will give you a dollar today.
But I expect that dollar to be $10,000 tomorrow.

MY MINDS EYE

MUSHROOMS

The mushrooms
cloud my brain as the silence and the noise tames
The part of me that says some are superior so naturally, there are inferiors.
Do you have a superiority complex? I hold my breath. You let it rip with your
misogynist business, plan to count me out. I see your cigarette, you've
offered me a puff but I've had enough, this shit is rough. I dance to the beat of
fallen raindrops of black soot. That go kaput with every remark that they are
worthless, lazy, and worthy of prison. Prison, as a state of mind. Free yourself
from confined thoughts that black soot isn't clean enough. It runs down my
back and through my spine in 200 years of
sooty lines. I am brain drain from the
African continent. Drained of juice and
spirit and youth. I am strong, I promise. I
am conditioned to accept, consent,
contempt, and repent, That black soot that
clouds the American mind that
says in plain English that "my kind"
is worthless and unworthy of respect or love.
Education that flourishes like doves that are
Released from the cage of a U.S. zoo stage.
But the mushrooms cloud my brain and I dance,
and dance, and dance in the rain of black soot
Infested with those who
took their fists and said
"fuck this shit. We deserve to die
and fly but try." Free from the cloudy
days that rain on our parades. Of chemicals
that burn acid in the flesh that was once so fresh.

Free, free,
we run in the streets. Naked and screaming
And glittered in gold for we are pharaohs and sphinxes with kingdoms so
bold. And we know our worth, our love and the Earth so our hearts erupt
with life and resiliency. As the gold pours from our pores, they call us eye
sores. But we love the chocolate and we love the
gold that we were told for so long to hide
and scold but no
longer will I hide.
I will fuck and eat
and cry. And smile
for a while. Because the
rainy black soot falls over me

And
For
once,

I am Free.

THE TRUTH

Oh, how I wish my life could be the same, after I heard what they do to people
like me.
Hang us from trees and let us fall like autumn leaves.
The rain pours down on the bodies that drown on blood clogged throats
From the cuts of those bloaks.

They hung the blacks with the same care that they would apply
To picture frames on walls:
delicate and planned.
Got to get rid of the crooked ones.
They threaten our vision of a white world,
with white walls, white stains, and white toy trains.
They hung the blacks with hate. Of course they wipe away the smudge
of an influential race. Seemingly good at everything.
Everything but staying safe. 'Cause the black smudge had too much Earth,
Too much birth, too much love.

We vote them in and blow love notes of change
While they walk us to our graves.
We are brave.
Fierce with hearts of gold
Or coal is what we're told.
Fuck the lies of dead lilies and rotten flies,
We are the ones we've been waiting for.
I wait by the cellar door as they throw me in
and lock my hope outside and rot until my entire soul dies.

Who did they kill to become king of anything? Oh yeah,
The black bodies on the Christmas trees.
St. Nick brought an eternal debt to the rich.
He serves my backside. Sliced and diced and served with ice
so the elite can munch on the part of me that's the most appetizing.
Funny, how the body is a treat for them to eat

To leave out to rot like meat
That was too tough to swallow.
Swallow these black hole pits.
I get so restless with this pacifist shit.
Of the appropriation, adoration, and fascination
With real life shit they don't have to deal with.
Pay the price for a taste of poison that they eat in
small portions but feed to black bodies as entrees.
Go ahead, eat my poisoned ass. I'll poison you too.
For I am the toxic dump you bred me to be.

Eat our soak.
Swallow a coke.
Smoke a blunt for lunch.
Rock Nikes to the wedding brunch
And fuck a woman in her cunt and
tell her she asked for your piece of shit
lump full of STDs from cultures you take
and mistakes you make. Still no protection
For heaven's sake.
If you don't know what I mean, take the broken
glass you threw at me. If you're hanging from trees,
then you're with me.

ONE (PLANET)

"Free Bird"
Acrylic on Canvas
2017

DIRT FLOORS

Dirt floors in el campo
Remind me of sun pores when it's damp out.
They open up to release a piece of earth
and send it on its way to make a place somewhere else.
Where else than home? Hustling feet.
Bustling tostadas and tostones that wreak
of mother's sweat and lips wet with papaya juice
and sacred youth.

Home

Never felt so rich when I no longer had a fridge.
I've never felt so warm in a house with no hot water.
Or safe in a place with no security latch.

But we said,

"Mama, Lulu, we need more café.
This tastes like hot cocoa, we could drink this all day."
When we asked for more love, she said,
"Dime, hija. Te quiero como sería mi sobrina".
I lock these words away in my core
And gently let them sink into the dirt floor.
That way the Earth will soak them up
And take them to a place where they need more.

More.
More.
More.

We say this religiously as U.S. citizens.
Notice, we are not alone.

This whole hemisphere is full of Americans, who also say more.
But in a different vein.
For us to share is what they claim.

To share the Earth's fluid
And the capture of the sun.
Please don't share if it's war and guns.
Some have died too young.
I hear from the dirt stories.
Of the revolution and all of their worries.
Where's our revolution?
To give the words back to those who live
in dirt floor shacks.

APOYAME LAGUNA

MY MINDS EYE

I am a woman of the sea.
The laguna takes me
to a place of no fear.
Far, far away from here.
Away from the drugs,
the bodies and the crows,
away from the stuck up
kids with cocaine on their noses.
Away from the cheap
Facebook profile pose.
Of all those things only the laguna knows.

I breath in dirt and spit out gold.
They tell me I'll be happy
when I'm fat and old
with the wrinkles that tell time
and cataracts in my eyes.

Laguna de Apoyo
ayudame a llorar.
la rejeccion me corta,
yo sonaba de muerta.
Kings and Queens of
Laguna lake, I'll do
whatever it takes.
Take my hand and
drag me beneath.

I want to feel the fishies
swim in between my teeth.
I'll be smiling
as I lay in the reef.

For on land,
the people are as hot
and rigid as sand
that burns my feet.

It's fine if its not the right time.
I just thought ocean love
would taste real sweet.

Like milk for a baby.
Like sun when it's real shady.
Like love when there's no price.
Like the perfect combo of
sweetness and spice.
Like the trees that smell of evergreen
and the knowledge there no "I" in team.

Laguna de Apoyo. Por qué no
¿Apoyamos al otro?
¿Por qué no piensan como nosotros?
¿Porque no pueden salir?
¿Y entonces no necesitamos escuchar?
Termina tus impresiones
Actitudes y suposiciones.
You don't know me
and you don't know the sea.

As far as I'm concerned,
you don't know anything.
All you know is what it's
like to have it easy.

Before you cast your opinion,
open up your eyes,
To see that indeed
the ocean cries.
And the ignorance
is what carries lies
Across the sea and
fed to the flies.

HOME

The sun never slept and neither did I.
It was light the whole time
as Europe layover the horizon.
I'm not sure if from the plane looking out
that I am looking at water or petrified sea.
It's beauty enchants me
with curves and textures
That remind me of
Fresh ice cream back home.

Home

Home

Home

Twenty days until I see Colorado prairie.
You know, the way it used to be before
they put a McDonald's on the wildflowers.

Home

Home

Home

The feeling I get when I feel the heat
of the shower on my neck
And my feet melt from underneath me.
The warmth of the shower brings me
to my knees like Kyptonite
in broad daylight.
Like the warmth you get
when the sun never slept.

Home
Home
Home

Sometimes it makes me cold.
Shivering sweat in the cold night.
Like the feeling of stepping out
of the shower. Like Icelandic
raindrops on my scalp.
I call for help
But it doesn't exist.
Only once per day
every 3 months
when school's out.

Home
Home
Home

Is it possible that home
is not in Colorado?
That the rock cliffs
that separate me from the west,
and the grassy McDonald's plains
that separate me from the east,
are not normal, average things?
Should I explore, implore, galore
at places that are not rocky waterfalls
pitfalls and know-it-alls?
Is there something over the horizon
that I cannot see?
That place over there where
the sun is glistening? Or
is that the fluffy cloud
water giving me a run
for my money?

MY MINDS EYE

Home

Home

Home

I'll find you someday.
Beyond the borders
of the U.S., I'm sure
is where I belong.
For now, I shall sing
Icelandic songs of
yore, every so patriotically .
At least until I get to
Amsterdam.

MY MINDS EYE

(BLACK) FEMINISM

"Begin Again"
Acrylic on Canvas
2018

WHAT IS FEMINISM?

I'm high as a kite but my wings
are clipped thin. The female must
always fly
regardless of her condition. She must
survive with the offspring. Why do we
have
to be so
strong?
Fierce as
oxen but
soft as
lotion.

MY MINDS EYE

I AM MAMA

Bearer of the bodies
Goddess of the sun.
Respectful matron of light and love.
Mama, I am you.
Your chocolate hands blend with the Earth's soil.
You bring light green sprouts to plant
in your own mother.
She closes her womb around the life
and nurtures its growth
from seedling to bud to plant to harvest.
Mama, you are the meaning of life.
The giver of love, nutrients, and light.
Where would we be without you?
Cold, hungry, hurting.
Mama, please forgive me for overutilizing your soil.
I know you can only give so much
before you become exhausted.
I am in my plant phase, mama.
If you carry me a little further,
I will bring you a harvest in return.

HOLD THE WEIGHT

It must feel like 1000 pounds, mama.
All the weight you carry.
Your weight.
My weight.
Their weight.
Your job's weight.
The weight of marriage.
The weight of disappointment.
The weight of bills.
The weight of oppression.
The weight of womanness.
The weight of blackness.
The weight of history.
The weight of herstory.
The weight of the present.
The weight of the future.
We can't all be weightless, mama.
But I'd like to help.

BEING BLACK IN A COLORADO COLLEGE TOWN WHILE YOU'RE DRINKING YOUR JUICE

MY MINDS EYE

It's amazing the alienation
I feel in this space.
White faces pass, I step on the breaks
and let go of the gas.
I'm stuck between a hard place and a rock.
It's a shock how brainwashed they made us.
To see me,
see black and free
and wonder how I got to this place.
They grimace at my intelligence,
curse at the opportunities I am granted,
and associate me with poverty and gangs.
How can you be so afraid?
You act like a victim now I want to treat you like one.
Oops, there I go again.
Fitting snuggly into the box they put me in.
What do you expect when I've been caged up
and treated like an animal?
All of us have.
For 200 years.

Yeah, I'm gonna bite your ass
and watch as you shed tears.
I feel nothing when white tears fall.
Oh well, they don't see
my black tears at all.
They see deserving of pain and undeserving of pleasure.
Leisure as lazy and death as inevitable.
The blues eyes watch me as I walk up the steps.
They burn holes in my chest.
They think they're the best
with Eurocentric ignorance.
Never considering their superiority complex.
I head west and lay on the coast
Next to a bloak from Berkeley.
Blue-eyed Kentucky boy with a chocolate fetish.
Living next to my brothers starving
to get on the next train out of here.
Yet locked up again in a place with no trains,
a place with brains that uses their privilege
to elevate their own gains.
I tear out my heart and throw it to the sky
and watch as carrier pigeons clip one piece
and send it on it's way.
Everyday I live with lies they tell.
That black is hell,
that brown is lowdown,
and white and rich is happiness,
That black and woman is the perfect excuse
for exploitative action.
That black and woman don't need
Care,
Love,
Support,
Kisses,
Lunch,
Love,
Partners,
Money,

MY MINDS EYE

Love,
Compassion,
Action,
Love,
A car,
A mom,
We need exactly what you need.
A chance to live,
a chance to breathe,
space to be free
in this golden brown blanket
I was wrapped in as a child.
Smooth and mild cocoa chips
with shea butter lips.
We need each other.
to be breathe our collective sigh of revival.

MY MINDS EYE

DON'T PASS THE BALL

Don't pass the ball
When you have it all.
You're right in front of the goal.
You know your role.
Score!
Mete!

You're the winner, darling.
Feminista chica,
Have some confianza.
His beard, his voice
is not the only choice.
You're right in front.
You have the intelligence.
Don't let it go to waste.

You pass the ball
When the light is on you.
Don't let his voice crowd
your 9th cloud.
Don't huff and puff,
kick it in the butt.
Feminista chica,
I cheer for you.
Jumping up and down,
I look like a fool.

When you pace yourself,
take a breath.
And pass the ball
to your left.

Be strong, be proud
Be smart, be loud!
Let the flowers flow,
you know it's a go.
Jump right in.
Give it a shot
But by god,

Don't
Let
The
Beard
Win.

MY MINDS EYE

DON'T TOUCH

You wouldn't
touch a bee
hive without
expecting to
be stung. You
wouldn't smoke
a cigarette with
-out knowing there
would be poison
in your lungs. And
you wouldn't touch
a woman. Without consent unless you we expecting to get away scath-free.
Well I am here to explain: When you touch a woman without consent, Expect
for you dick to be clipped And hung for the bees to sting and the flies to eat
and the maggots to chomp while we stand and watch. Take your dirty paws
off my ass or your jaw will end up like broken glass. Run your hand up my
spine one more time and I'll break each one of your fingers. All in a line.
Consent, motherfucker. Educate yourself. Imagine how you would have felt.
Someone grabs your dick, tickles it and calls it a shrimp. Someone saunters
up to you, slips a roofie in your drink, tells people you made sweet, sweet
love then you literally feel fucked and don't remember a thing. All you
fuckers who get away scath-free. Fuck that, now is my time to go free. Let
out all of the bullshit and pain you've caused me. And all of you who think
it's okay to touch a black woman's afro, allow me to inform you,
It's not.

Don't touch without consent
Or you're next.
Xoxo

WHEN I WAS HER

When I was Her
Scared of the
The chatter that
negative noth
Whispers that
and hijacked
a stolen train.

I was scared
noise in my head.
whispered sweet
-ings in my brain.
stole my courage
my dreams like
When I was Her.

I dreamt of a life of freedom. One where money
flowed into my bank account and all I had to do
was be myself. When I was her, myself wasn't
enough, the chatter in my head tried to run from
it. You are
the mirror.
consumed me.
vision into a
Is it me or her

enough I said in
But the mirror
Turned every
distant fantasy.
that I'm looking at

Was this a reflection of the past? My eyes twitch
and fall through my consciousness and come out
on the other side. Come alive I told myself.
Swallowed my pride and
put my doubts on the shelf.
Sat down and thought to myself. This
is it. The 9-5 has got to go. Your chains
need to be gone. You need to be in
your flow. Don't
stop fighting for
that sweet taste of freedom. It's on your tongue.
And it tastes as sweet and forbidden as bubble-
gum when you were young. When you were young.

It's so sweet. Taste it and let your dreams
treat you to the bitterness that comes with free
-dom. Regret, disappointment, failure, they will come
for you. But you, are not there. When I was her. I would
fear the taste of   bubblegum. Sweet
and forbidden. But   in my mind, it was
just the beginning.   When the taste
becomes real, do not resist.
 All that's left is   the shell of her.
 Let her rest.   And become you.
 The you with   stars in your eyes
 and no time to   r   e   s   t.

QUEER (LIBERATION)

"In My Kingdom"
Acrylic on Wood
2015

QUEER FREEDOM

Queer freedom looks like...

Bumps and bodies,
blazers embellished with burgundy bow ties
blowing bubbles in a beautiful ballet ballroom.

Sweet, salty and sassy queers
in sensational sued slacks
Symbolically situated next to
sand castle soirees.

Livid, lovely, loosely liable lovers living lives to the last breath.
Lace and latex without longing for legitimate legislation
to offer them any legal protections.
Lovers in memory lane.

With freedom songs
on their tongues
and social protection
tying their torsos
together.

936 EUDORA

I saw the makeup. Blues, purples, yellows.
Splattered on the walls of the backdrop,
On mannequin heads.
I take the yellow and write "prodigy"
on my forehead.
I learned from my role models.
Models of genders beyond the spectrum
And in the outer space of the binary system.
The yellow, clouds my gaze and faux tits
make their debut in my living room.
Hair, pimples, and concealer work
together. They form sunshine and rainbows.
Bows with polka dots, silk and jewels lined on panties
on non-conforming bodies.
Bodies in space.
Holding each other's astronomically blue epithets.
Blue skies line the Colorado atmosphere
as blue glitter lines their nostrils.
Blue table stands hold fresh mints and plastic orchids
designed to be inviting to the plastic feminine bodies on my couch.
The couch holds memory parcels of late night movie series.
Too Wong Foo, Thanks for Everything, Julie Newmar;
Priscilla, Queen of the Desert;
Paris is Burning.
Boiling in purple satin is a queen bee
who doesn't take no for an answer.
Purple lipstick lines her lips
and smudges her finger tips.
Purple hearts in the air
as the heir of her throne
touches her lips.

Purple lenses capture their kiss.
I rise with eyes full of
rainbow stilletos
rainbow trapezes
rainbow clitori
rainbow penises
rainbow stars at
rainbow nightclub bars.

The young girl in me
finds what it means
to be a women in
this world. From the
nude-colored tits in
the corner. And the
strap-on in the upstairs
closet.

MY MINDS EYE

THE DIFFERENCE BETWEEN HOT AND BEAUTIFUL

MY MINDS EYE

Sometimes I wish I was hot and sometimes I wish I was beautiful.
The eyes burn holes in my back and my heart shines through
my chest like it's trying to keep track of who I am.
To me, hot and beautiful can't be measured, weighed or gained,
lost or trained, bought or claimed. It's the way the heart shines
seen through another's eyes. To be hot or beautiful are not
one in the same. If you were confused, you are not to blame they are
used as terms to be interchanged.
If you give me a chance I'd like to explain:

HOT	BEAUTY
Hot is controllable.	Beauty is intangible.
Hot is temporary.	Beauty is everlasting.
Hot is a craze.	Beauty can amaze.
Hot is painful to the touch.	Beauty is warm enough.
Hot is a point in time.	Beauty cannot be quantified
Hot is a glimpse of your chest.	Beauty is the wind from your breath
Hot is when it snaps.	Beauty is when it collapses
Hot is sex.	Beauty is complex
Hot is when you make it clap.	Beauty is when food falls in your lap.

As you can see,
hot is obvious,
beauty is androgynous.

Hot is when the strap of your dress
falls off of your shoulder,
and the front of your chest
tells me its getting a little colder,
and the hair on your legs
tell me you're a little Boulder
than I thought you were.
Beauty is when you stand before me,
and your eyes, arms, legs, feet, I can see
and you see I'm watching
and you're getting sweaty
but that's okay because
you feel pretty.
Sometimes I wish I was hot
Sometimes I wish I was beautiful.
Oh well, all I can be is me
with my eyes, arms, legs, feet
and heart for you to see.

MY MINDS EYE

PHILO (SOPHY)

TIME

The time moves
like a cherry-lime icey in June.
But it's November and slow,
that's as far as it'll go.

I wish the time would never end
to stop the way a body bends.
Come on youth flow right through,
bring with you a bag of new.
I'll need it when I see the true,
meaning of life is to work and die.
When all you've known was a lie
and when you look up to the sky,
all you see are suits and ties
and butterflies that flutter by
with eyes of pain and wings with chains,
confined to debt from corporate gains.

As you stare, you see how insane
the way we live without our brains.
We work to live and say we tried
but move one inch with every stride.
Yet we swim and sink in the tide,
the gasp for air won't let us survive.
We bubble and splash beneath the sea
of green trees and corporate greed.
As we sink, we then go poof
and we return to our youth,
where we find that the whole time,
the way to live was to free our minds
of time.

THE BEST THINGS IN LIFE AREN'T PERFECT

Sudoku is hard as shit.
I get so frustrated when the puzzle isn't perfect.
The right answer, isn't hard to find.
I try to focus my mind to make sense
of numbers and shapes.
Patterns and escapes.
No one said every puzzle was the same.
I try to keep sane but some puzzles are hard to resolve.
Like the tablets I put in water
that are supposed to dissolve.

This obsession is sickness.
Imperfection is not weakness.
The puzzle of life, to live well and eat right,
are privileges and kites of the elite in the world.
But money is not what makes you poor or rich.
Happiness is not if you fit into this niche.
Security is not determined by a push or a click.
They told me to think like this
But it was all a trick.
The truth is, the best things in life aren't perfect.
Immaculate, expensive or worth it.
The best things in life are things without a price.
Hair without lice.
Sunsets are nice.
The day you met your wife.
Kids without knives.
Peace would suffice.
I'm talking about things
Without factoring in economics,
Politics or trigonomics.

The things you can I take for granted.
All the things we've ever wanted.

But I love the way you look when I share.
All of the imperfect things I have because I care.
Broke and belittled.
Irregular, rectangular,
poetry and riddles.
That's what I can offer.
is my love an my rhyme.
For I am a person who is
Broke and blind.
I say the best things in life aren't perfect,
Like you and me and things that aren't worth it
But before I go,
I want you to know:
This poem is imperfect.
And that's my favorite kind of way
to spend my today
with you.

MY MINDS EYE

COLOR

There's something peculiar about colour.
It paints the outer layer a hue of value.
Red: brilliant, sexy, spontaneous.
White: Innocent, simple, delicate.
Black: ... but what is black?
Evil, deceptive, dark?
Truly none of that.
Black is simply
Neutral.
A colour
of
quiet.
It's the color
one sees when their eyes collapse.
It's the color one sees when the sun is shot from
the sky. Black is not a threat. Black is not an enemy.
Black is neutral.
Black is beautiful.

HEART (BREAK)

"Fuck You, Thank You"
Acrylic on Canvas
2018

FUCK YOU,THANK YOU

MY MINDS EYE

Fuck you for leaving me.
Like a puppy in a box on the side of highway.
Like I never happened, like you never wanted me.
Fuck you for showing me how deep my ego is and how sensitive my heart is.
I wish you hadn't played games and used my emotional energy to make
yourself feel better.
I wish you hadn't given me the high of my life
by sweeping me up in your arms like the mess I knew I was
and making me feel like I could be clean and pure again.
Fuck you for showing how beautiful I was naked
but not beautiful enough to be your forever.
You know, what?

Thank you.

Thank you for leaving me like a puppy in a box on the side of the highway
So finally, I could feel what it's like to be free of the expectation
To be cute and small and harmless so finally I can roam the streets
like the alpha bitch I knew I always was.
Your neglect brought freedom.
Your abandonment brought strength.
You brought the worst crush to my ego
But the greatest excuse to rise from the ashes
Like a fucking phoenix.
Sometimes we have to fall to realize
we've always been good enough
strong enough, powerful enough for ourselves.
And saying fuck you and thank you are not contradictions,
rather, the same message wrapped in two different packages
Catch and release.

Hold, crush and be the diamond
from the pressure of being a rock.
From being the truth.
From being the person I always was
Without you.
Without you.
And without you.

Fuck you,
Thank you.

Fuck you for using me.
Thank you for leaving me.
Fuck you for kissing me like I was the most beautiful thing.
Thank you for reminding me that your lips meant nothing to me.
Could not break me,
stomp me or stop me.
Thank you for stopping me
when I fell for you
because you knew how garbage you were
and how I never needed to clean you up.
Fuck you for loving me,
making me feel like I needed you,
like I couldn't breath with you,
like I couldn't see without you,
like I was blind.
Like love always is.
Thank you for reminding me how little I need besides myself.
How extracurricular you are to my happiness.
How distracting you are to my sense of divinity.
How my holiness and halo are not gone because you stole them,
but because I realized I don't need your validation to be a goddess
in my own eyes,
in my size 4 thighs,
in my golden tear drop dries.
That my sense of divinity
will and can never be taken
by a man, a devil or you (both).
My humanity will not be diminished
by your inability to see me as a queen.
So fuck you, thank you
Fuck,
Thank you.

REVIVAL

Today was a revival
I survived the thrill of hating him.
Wanting to skin him and wear him
like a poor quality Russian mink.
But I remembered I'm vegan
and that's probably unethical and shit.
But forget it.
I survived.
I've had a revival.
I've turned my rival
into an archival piece
of my honorary ex-boyfriend library.
Lucky him.
Seems like it's time to clean the stacks
and throw some into the trash.
Not every memory is worth saving.
Not every partner is worth craving.
But he, my Russian mink monster,
wreaked of falsehoods.
Fake everything from the outside in.
Fearful of sin but let lust control his every action.
Fucking strangers and blaming them
for taking his ticket to heaven away.
Never did he take responsibility
for his own drama.
Rather, it was always someone else's
fault, locking away his shame in a vault.
With one code to get in:
accepting that sin is in his head.
And he let the fear of HIM control every whim.
When will he grow up to realize:
we may use God as an excuse to guide us

but we need to draw the line
when you're not able to distinguish
your choices from those you call sin.
Call it what it is.
Your own fear, hesitations
and short comings.
Don't come here no more.
Don't knock on my door
and ask for me.
I'm not there.
I'm living my life like
there's nothing there to stop me.
While you're praying to a God
that may never answer your prayers.
Pray to him like he's the answer.
Fall to your knees and ask
for forgiveness.
Ask for him.
Not me.
I'm in revival.

MY MINDS EYE

IN THE LION'S DEN

In darkest corner,
I see his teeth glow
behind those Rastafarian dreads.
Glowing in the night like lights
wanting to do me in.
But I won't let them.
Oh, I've been her before.
The Rastafari on the beach
in Nica once swayed me
like a palm in the wind
overlooking the Pacific Ocean.
It felt forbidden.
But so right from the beginning.
Bonfire led to Bob Marley
on a beach bungalow
blowing and baking ourselves like brownies.
A cloud of clownies
from my sophomore class
blow kisses my way.
I sway
and fall into his dreadlocked lion's den.
I'll never forget the glow in his teeth
made of knives.
I lift my eyes and see a pack.
They laugh like hyenas
on the safari outback.
Playing djembe
and making copper rings 'n tings.
They try to seduce me.
But little do they know
I've seen the lion's stare before.
The one where
they make your body into food,
your soul into a cheap drink,

your hair into spider webs
for their fingers to get tangled in.
Your heart is a beating drum
that they can play
like the djembe in the den.
Fleeting women are fireflies
worthy of a catch.
They put out their lion paws
only to be swiping so fast
and viciously
the fireflies escape
into the Montezuma bosque, we go.
Into the clouds, into the sea.
Away from the hungry Rasta lions
den where so many fireflies like me
were put out.
Out of light.
High and dry.

MY MINDS EYE

STILL(NESS)

STILLNESS

I let each phalange on my foot
touch the floor one step at a time.
I let my limb move 2 miles per hour.
I let my spine articulate an undulation, slowly.
Stillness.
Stillness.
Stillness.
A beautiful rendition of wisdom and courage.
I feel like my grandmother in stillness.
I feel like an embodiment of time.
I am my grandmother.
I am time.
Slow
Old.
And wise.

MY MINDS EYE

BONUS POEM

"Habibi"
Acrylic on Canvas
2018

HABIBI

Habibi. How could you do this to me,
leave me in the desert and
watched me sink into earth.
I washed up, distraught and shocked.
I trusted your voice.
It's sweet noise reminded me
of the sand in the Middle East.
Blowing gently in the wind, silent and serene.
Remind me, why I fell for you?
Fell into your sand dune and nearly died.
Left my pride and ran into your eyes.
I closed the door behind me
despite the red flags that waved around me.
I entered your heart and fell into your soul.
You told me lies that I couldn't deny.
But I was blind by the oasis of you.
The water you represented in my desolate heart.
In you, I found meaning.
I found love and worth.
When you left, you stole that too.
My unreasonable heart and all that I knew.
For weeks, I sat in the dark.
Pulled myself out and left my heart with you.
You took my organ out of my beating chest
but all that remained was the dry red sand that you left.

THE END

Made in the USA
Middletown, DE
09 August 2019